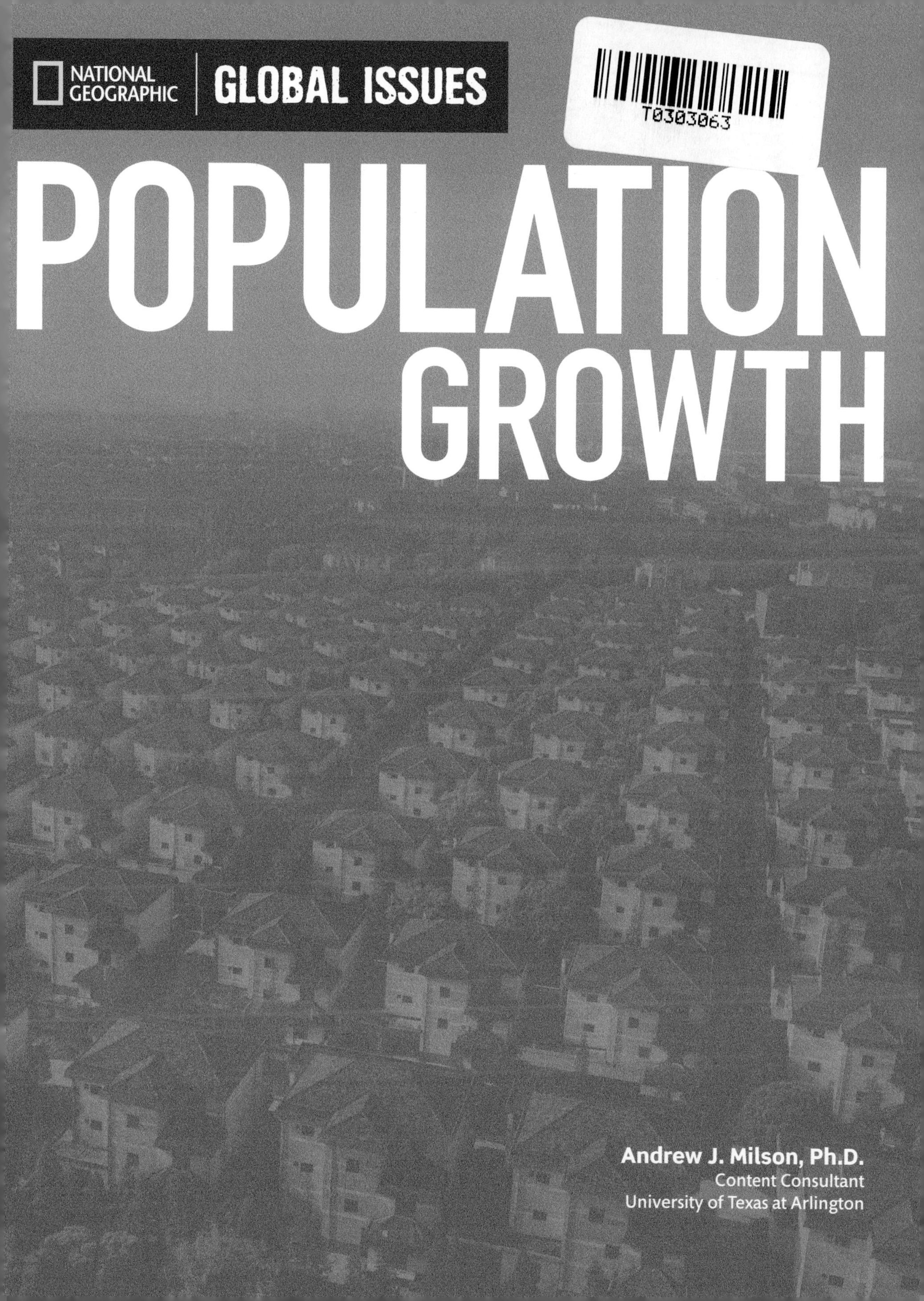

NATIONAL GEOGRAPHIC | GLOBAL ISSUES

POPULATION GROWTH

Andrew J. Milson, Ph.D.
Content Consultant
University of Texas at Arlington

NATIONAL GEOGRAPHIC LEARNING | CENGAGE Learning

Acknowledgments

Grateful acknowledgment is given to the authors, artists, photographers, museums, publishers, and agents for permission to reprint copyrighted material. Every effort has been made to secure the appropriate permission. If any omissions have been made or if corrections are required, please contact the Publisher.

Instructional Consultant: Christopher Johnson, Evanston, Illinois

Teacher Reviewers:
Linda O'Connor, Northeast Independent School District, San Antonio, Texas
Leah Perry, Exploris Middle School, Raleigh, North Carolina

Text Credits

15 Excerpt from "Seoul Ascending" by John Bowe from the *New York Times*, September 23, 2010. Copyright © 2010 by the New York Times. Reprinted by permission of the New York Times. All rights reserved.

Photographic Credits

Front Cover, Inside Front Cover, Title Page ©Randy Olson/National Geographic Stock. **4** (bg) ©Randy Olson/National Geographic Stock. **6** (bg) ©Claudio Gallone/agefotostock. **8** (bg) Mapping Specialists. **10** (bg) ©David White/Alamy. **11** (br) ©Kyung-sook Schoenman. **12** (t) ©Topic Photo Agency IN/agefotostock. **14** (bg) ©Leon Chew. **16** (bg) ©David Bathgate/Corbis. **17** (br) ©James P. Blair/National Geographic Stock. **19** (bg) ©Rafiqur Rahman/Reuters/Corbis. **20** (bg) ©Jenny Matthews/Alamy. **22** (bg) ©Jim Richardson/National Geographic Stock. **23** (bl) ©Jim Richardson/National Geographic Stock. **24** (t) ©Jim Richardson/National Geographic Stock. **27** (t) ©Radius/SuperStock. **28** (tr) ©RJW/The Image Bank/Getty Images. **30** (tr) ©Thomas Kokta/Peter Arnold/Getty Images. (br) ©Jenny Matthews/Alamy. **31** (bg) ©Matti Niemi/Folio Images/Getty Images. (tr) ©Jim Richardson/National Geographic Stock. (br) ©Matiullah Achakza/epa/Corbis. (bl) ©Topic Photo Agency IN/agefotostock.

Visit National Geographic Learning online at www.NGSP.com.

Visit our corporate website at www.cengage.com.

ISBN: 978-0-7362-9781-3

Printed in Mexico
Print Number: 08 Print Year: 2024

Introducing the ISSUE

A CROWD Planet

The streets of Kolkata, India, are filled with vehicles, pedestrians, and street vendors. This bustling city has nearly 4.5 million inhabitants.

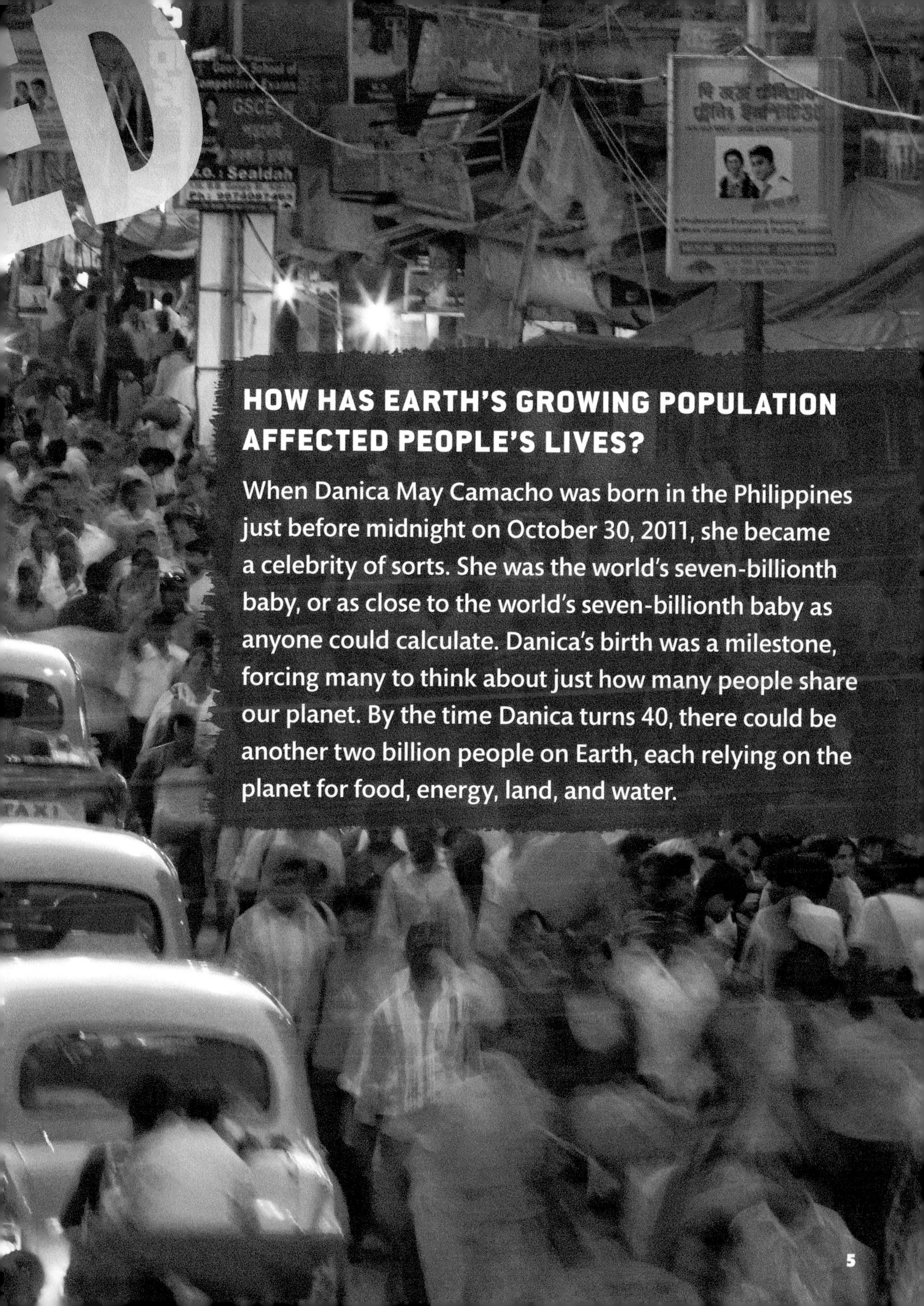

HOW HAS EARTH'S GROWING POPULATION AFFECTED PEOPLE'S LIVES?

When Danica May Camacho was born in the Philippines just before midnight on October 30, 2011, she became a celebrity of sorts. She was the world's seven-billionth baby, or as close to the world's seven-billionth baby as anyone could calculate. Danica's birth was a milestone, forcing many to think about just how many people share our planet. By the time Danica turns 40, there could be another two billion people on Earth, each relying on the planet for food, energy, land, and water.

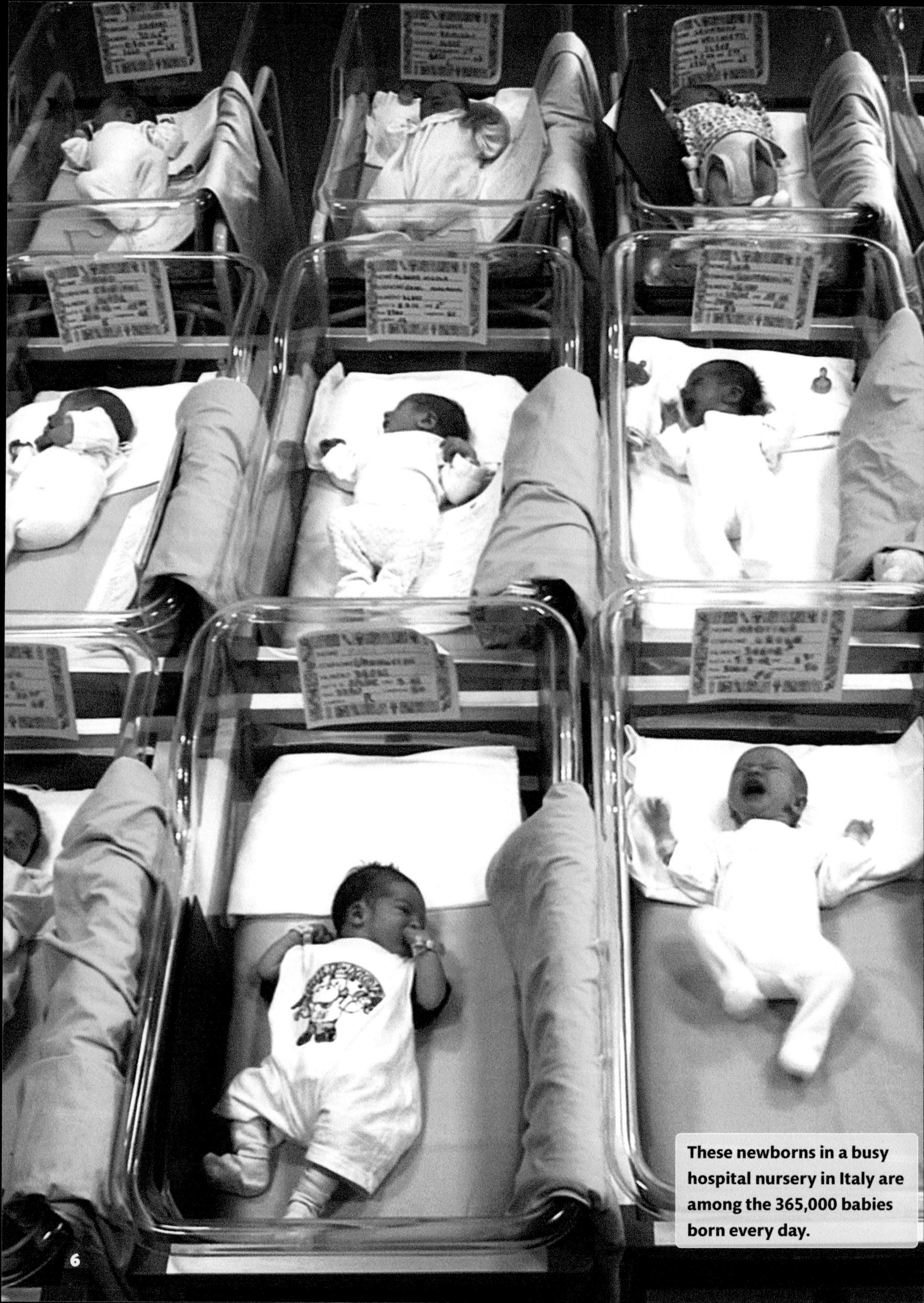

These newborns in a busy hospital nursery in Italy are among the 365,000 babies born every day.

SEVEN BILLION AND COUNTING

Population is the total number of people who occupy an area. Earth's large population is in some ways a sign of our success. It means we're living longer because of good medical care and a high standard of living. Only 60 years ago, the average human lifespan was 48 years. Today it's over 65.

Earth wasn't always crowded. According to some estimates, around 10,000 years ago there were fewer than 10 million people. Then, as advances in technology, farming, medicine, and other areas began to take hold, the human population started to grow.

Nearly 300 years ago people started eating better and taking new medicines to control disease. As a result, the rate of population growth ballooned. World population reached one billion in the 1800s and doubled to two billion in the early 1900s. In the 100 years since then, we've added five billion more people. Each day 365,000 babies are born.

ENOUGH FOR EVERYONE?

The growing population puts an ever-increasing strain on the planet. Vital resources such as food, water, and energy are being consumed at an alarming rate. This struggle is not shared equally. Wealthier countries tend to consume many resources faster than they can be replaced. Meanwhile, nearly one billion people don't have enough to eat, and 900 million don't have enough clean water to drink.

In some places, resources have become so scarce that people have to **migrate**, or move somewhere else, to survive, creating problems in the countries the migrants move to. The growing population also means that some countries face economic ruin because they are taking care of so many more elderly, poor, and sick people. As you will learn, South Korea and Bangladesh are good examples of two different types of population challenges.

Explore the Issue

1. **Find Main Idea and Details** What are two reasons why the human population has grown?
2. **Form and Support Opinions** Is population growth mainly positive or negative for humans?

Impact of Populatior

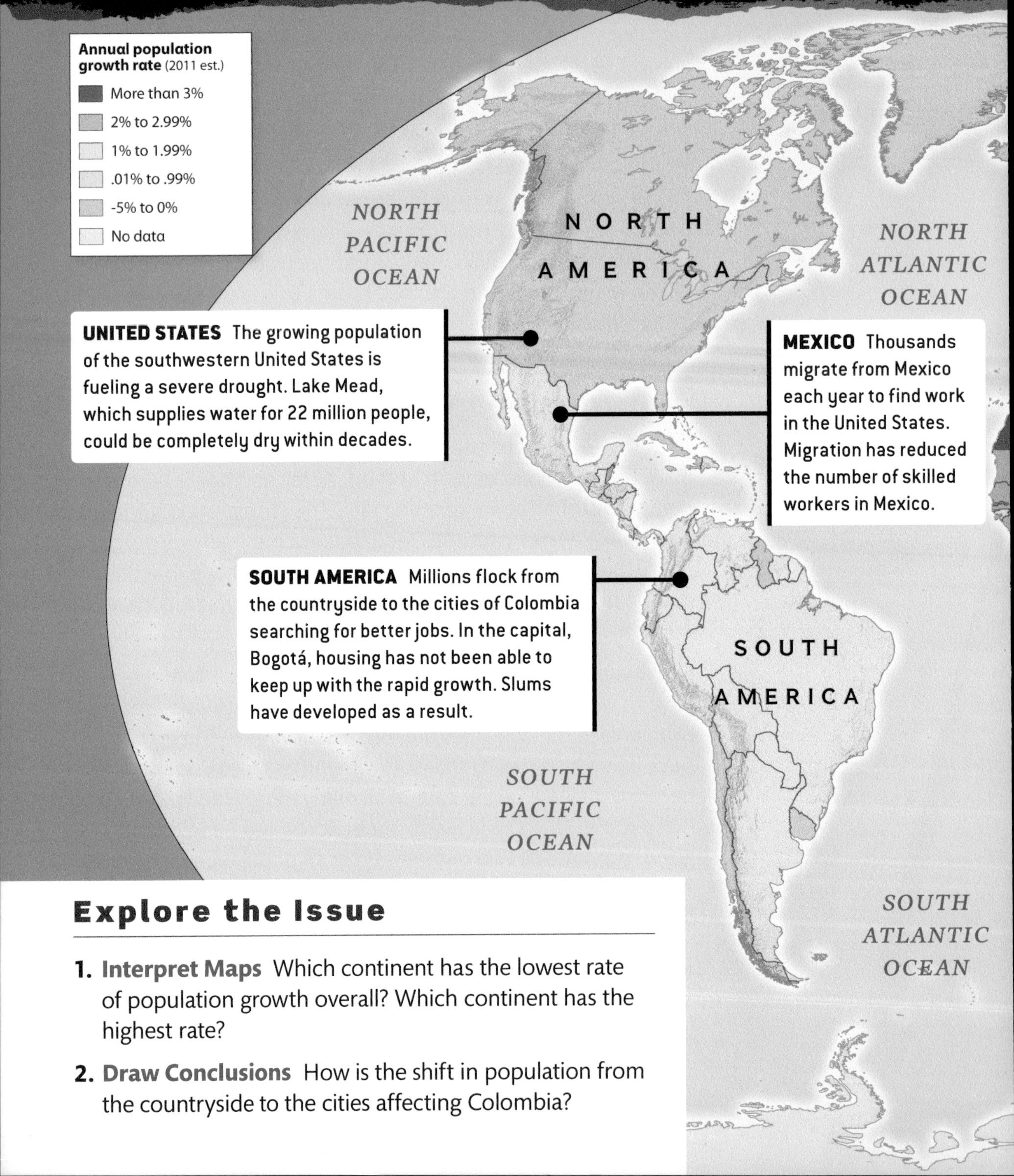

UNITED STATES The growing population of the southwestern United States is fueling a severe drought. Lake Mead, which supplies water for 22 million people, could be completely dry within decades.

MEXICO Thousands migrate from Mexico each year to find work in the United States. Migration has reduced the number of skilled workers in Mexico.

SOUTH AMERICA Millions flock from the countryside to the cities of Colombia searching for better jobs. In the capital, Bogotá, housing has not been able to keep up with the rapid growth. Slums have developed as a result.

Explore the Issue

1. **Interpret Maps** Which continent has the lowest rate of population growth overall? Which continent has the highest rate?
2. **Draw Conclusions** How is the shift in population from the countryside to the cities affecting Colombia?

Growth

Study the map below to learn how the world's increasing population affects countries in different parts of the world.

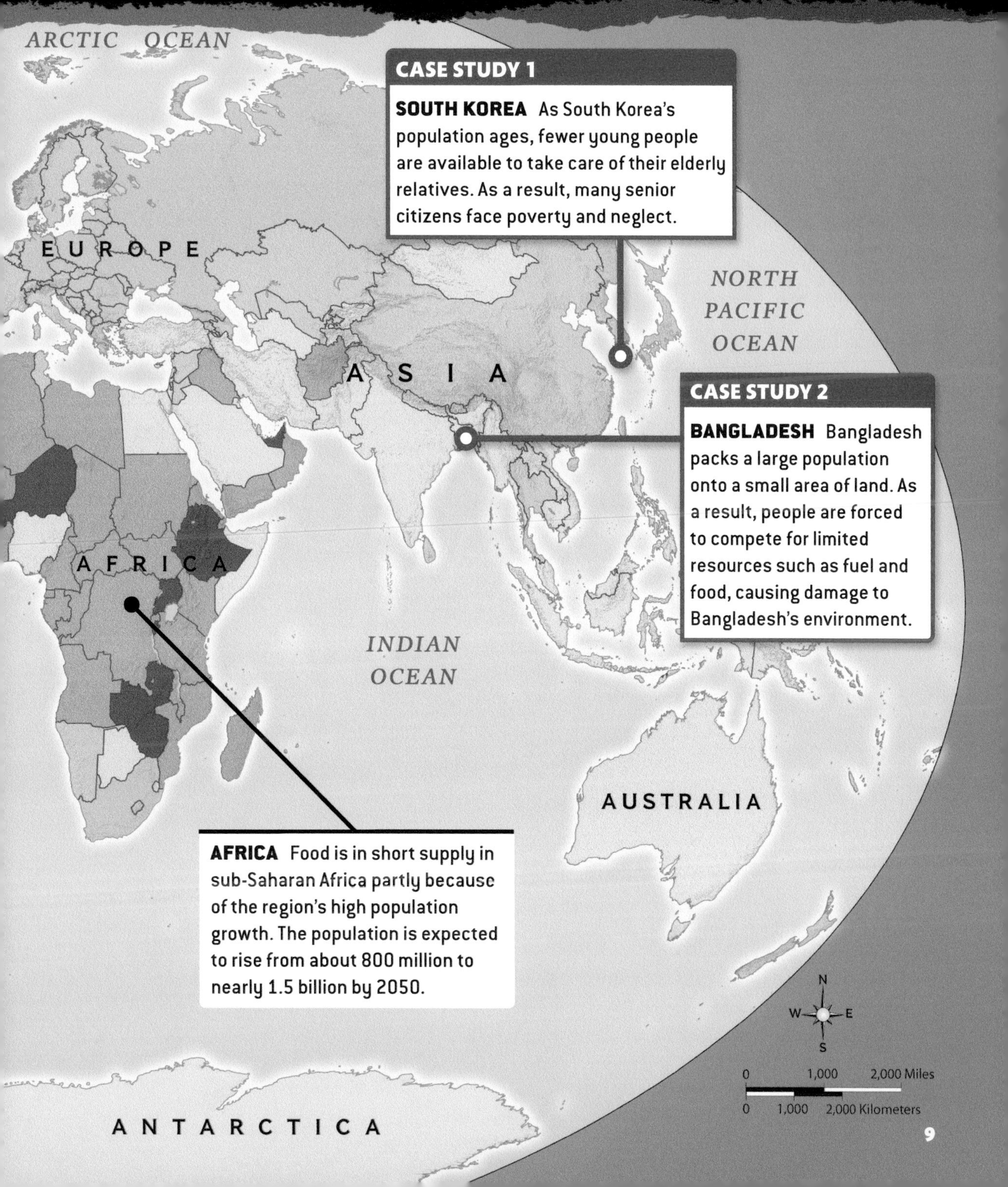

CASE STUDY 1

SOUTH KOREA As South Korea's population ages, fewer young people are available to take care of their elderly relatives. As a result, many senior citizens face poverty and neglect.

CASE STUDY 2

BANGLADESH Bangladesh packs a large population onto a small area of land. As a result, people are forced to compete for limited resources such as fuel and food, causing damage to Bangladesh's environment.

AFRICA Food is in short supply in sub-Saharan Africa partly because of the region's high population growth. The population is expected to rise from about 800 million to nearly 1.5 billion by 2050.

Case Study ONE

SOUTH KOREA'S Aging Population

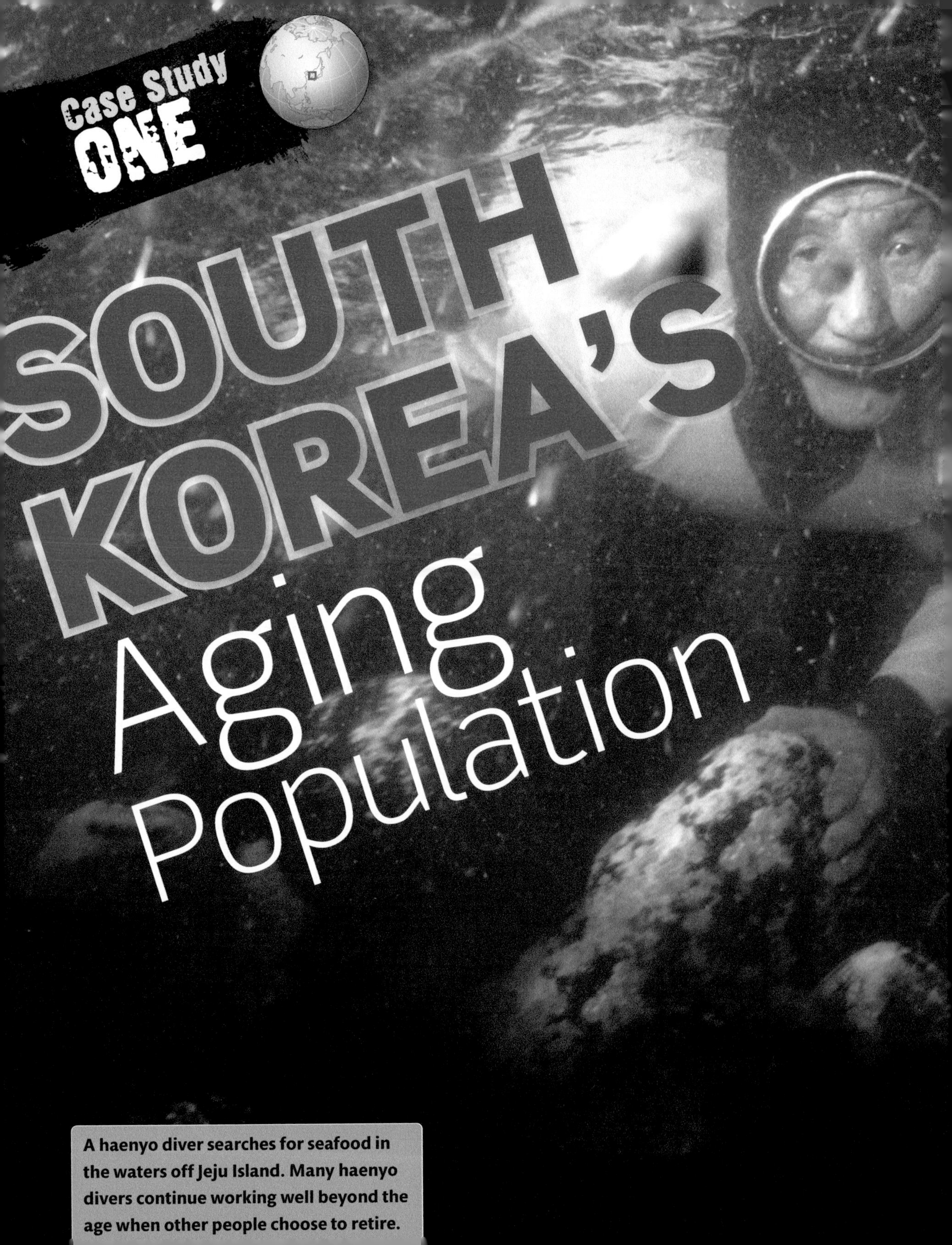

A haenyo diver searches for seafood in the waters off Jeju Island. Many haenyo divers continue working well beyond the age when other people choose to retire.

AGELESS WOMEN OF THE SEA

Every morning women on South Korea's Jeju Island put on their wet suits, sing a song, and then dive into the brisk waters of the Korean Strait. Known as *haenyo* (HAYN-yo), or sea women, these divers harvest octopus and large shellfish such as abalone from the ocean floor, a tradition passed from mother to daughter. Many of the divers are elderly. The haenyo continue diving well into their 70s.

These days, the haenyo way of life is in peril, threatened by modern fishing boats that intrude on the diving grounds and a younger generation that rejects the lifestyle. Diving in the haenyo style is, after all, dangerous and physically demanding. "One mistake and the ocean will kill you," says Kim Choun-geum, a 56-year-old haenyo. "Our rule is to never get greedy." Still, in a country where those 65 and older make up 11 percent of the population, the elderly haenyo seem to be South Korea's most active senior citizens.

The situation for older people in other parts of South Korea looks less rosy. The country's population is aging, and many older citizens live on limited incomes. These elderly must struggle to get by and to cope with living in cities that have become too crowded for comfort.

Haenyo divers take a boat to their fishing grounds.

This busy shopping district in Seoul (SOHL), South Korea's capital, illustrates two significant trends: the country's recent economic success and the overcrowding of its cities.

MANAGING CHANGE

In many ways, South Korea is thriving. Its economy has boomed in the past 20 years. However, the country faces two serious population issues: its aging citizens and its crowded cities. These trends are known as **demographic changes**—alterations in the size and makeup of a country's population.

South Korea's aging population is threatening to damage the country's economy. For one thing, the government's national pension plan is in trouble. People contribute to a national **pension plan** through their taxes. Then, when they retire, they receive regular payments from the plan to help them survive. With a large number of retired people receiving money from the pension plan and fewer younger workers paying taxes, the government's financial resources are becoming strained. In addition, because of South Korea's high cost of living, many adult children cannot afford to take care of their elderly parents.

At the same time, South Korea's birth rate is low, which means there will not be enough young people joining the workforce to replace the retirees who are leaving it.

A TOO SUCCESSFUL POPULATION POLICY

South Korea hasn't always had an aging population. In the early 1950s, South Korea was poor and rural, and the **fertility rate**—the average number of children born to each woman—was more than six. The population was growing rapidly.

As South Korea modernized, officials realized the mushrooming population was weakening the country's economic growth. Beginning in 1962, the government instituted several programs encouraging people to have fewer children.

The policy may have worked too well. As the country prospered, couples, especially those crowding into the cities, began having fewer children. Today South Korea has one of the lowest birth rates among the world's 30 most developed countries.

South Korea's government has started offering incentives for people to have more children. An **incentive** is a reward that is offered to encourage a certain behavior. For example, the government now gives families money for childcare to help ease the financial burden of having children.

The city of Seoul is a dense grid of housing and office towers. Between 1945 and today, Seoul's population has grown from around 1 million to more than 10 million people.

BRIGHT LIGHTS, CROWDED CITIES

The aging crisis is not South Korea's only demographic problem. After the Korean War (1950–1953), South Korea began to modernize, and its cities grew rapidly. Thousands of refugees moved into cities such as Seoul to seek shelter, as thousands more people from rural areas arrived seeking jobs. Today nearly 83 percent of South Koreans live in urban areas.

"We have a lot of people in such a small place, and we have to live together. If the factory is next door, making noise or pollution, you just have to learn to live with it," says Chun Sung-Myung, an artist who lives in Seoul.

Like the aging population, urban overcrowding is another problem the government has tried to solve by encouraging different behavior. In recent years, the government has focused on Seoul, where around a quarter of South Korea's population lives. For example, to tackle the problem of extreme vehicle congestion in the city, the government reformed and reorganized the public bus system. This encouraged more citizens to take the bus rather than their cars.

BALANCING IT OUT

Balance is the goal of all these efforts to influence the birth rate and urban population. A steady rate of population growth can help create a workforce that is balanced between older and younger workers. Creating a balance between urban and rural populations can ease the problems of overcrowded cities.

The final decisions, however, rest with individuals. Back on Jeju, home of the haenyo, many young people have moved to the mainland to find work. But Kim Jae-yeon (JAY YOON), South Korea's youngest haenyo, has stayed on, hoping to pass down the diving tradition to her 8-year-old daughter. "I'm already teaching her how to dive," she says. "Whether she wants to become a haenyo will be up to her."

Explore the Issue

1. **Find Main Ideas** What are two problems associated with South Korea's low birth rate?
2. **Analyze Cause and Effect** How has South Korea's economic growth affected its cities?

Case Study TWO

Banglades

A GROWING POPULATION IN A SHRINKING SPACE

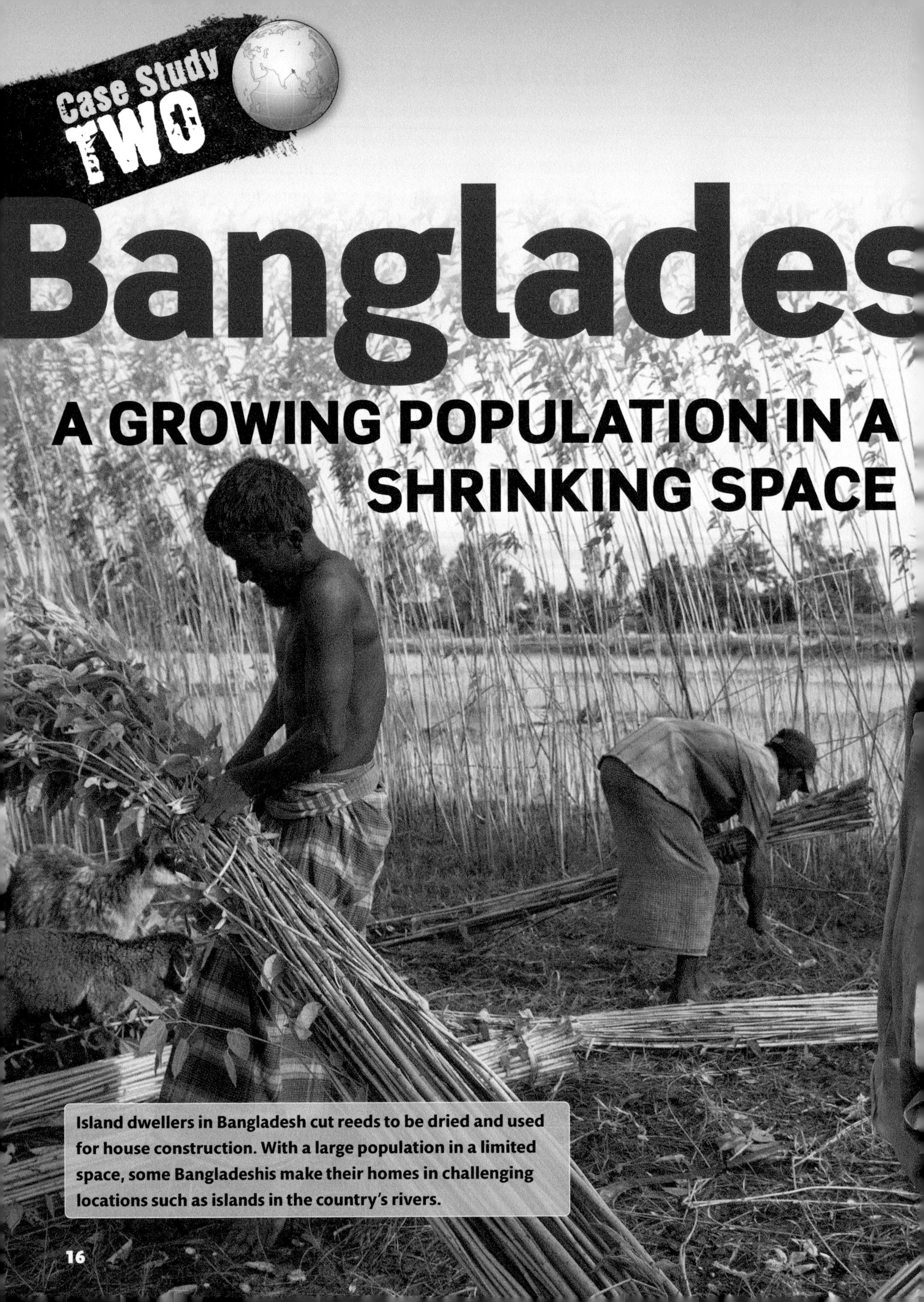

Island dwellers in Bangladesh cut reeds to be dried and used for house construction. With a large population in a limited space, some Bangladeshis make their homes in challenging locations such as islands in the country's rivers.

CHAR DWELLERS

Ibrahim Khalilullah (EE-brah-heem kah-lee-LOO-luh) has lost track of how many times he has moved over the years: 30? 40? 50? "Does it matter?" the 60-year old asks. Khalilullah is one of several hundred thousand people who live on the islands, or chars, on Bangladesh's major rivers. Floods and erosion often wash the islands away. When one island sinks, the char dwellers move to another. It's not unusual for a family to take their boat to go visit friends and discover that the char they were sailing to is no longer there. Later they will learn from the char-dwelling community where their friends have relocated.

"This is our only option, to move from place to place to place," Khalilullah says. "We farm this land for as long as we can, and then the river washes it away."

There are few places for Khalilullah and other char dwellers to live. With a population of 148 million crammed into a country slightly smaller than the U.S. state of Georgia, Bangladesh is a very crowded place. Because so many people are packed into such a small area, this tiny country has found itself at a dangerous intersection where a rapidly growing population and a fragile environment collide.

At Sadullapur, heavy rains caused the Meghna River to eat away at its banks, threatening homes. When people are forced from their homes, there is little space for them elsewhere in Bangladesh.

CHANGING ENVIRONMENT

Despite a sharp decline in its birth rate over the last 30 years, Bangladesh's population is likely to reach 200 million by 2050. All these people have to eat and live somewhere. The growing population creates an increasing demand for jobs, water, fuel, and shelter. Meeting these demands can cause harm to the environment. Overcrowded cities, with their factories and slums, use the country's rivers as open sewers, dumping chemicals, medical waste, human sewage, and other trash into the water.

In Dhaka (DAH-kuh), the capital, millions drink unsafe water from the Buriganga (boo-ree-GAHNG-uh), one of the most polluted rivers in the country. "The water of the Buriganga is now so polluted that all fish have died, and increasing filth and human waste have [turned it into] a black gel," says Ainun Nishat, an environmental expert. "Even rowing across the river is now difficult for it smells so bad." Millions of Bangladeshis depend on the country's 230 rivers, but many of these essential watercourses are drying up or being fouled by human construction and pollution.

ONE-TWO PUNCH

Experts warn that the situation can only get worse because of population growth and **climate change**, the gradual increase of Earth's surface temperature. Because 90 percent of Bangladesh is less than 33 feet above sea level, experts fear that rising sea levels fueled by climate change will flood two-thirds of the country, leaving people with no place to live or farm.

If that happens and the population swells toward the projected figure of 200 million, 10 to 30 million people will be forced to seek shelter inland or in neighboring India. Such a massive migration could cause major food and water shortages, an increase in disease, and political instability.

Bangladesh already knows what it's like to feel the one-two punch of population growth and environmental change. In recent years, natural disasters such as earthquakes, floods, and cyclones have uprooted millions, forcing many into overcrowded slums where the government cannot provide the most basic services.

After a flood in July 2007, villagers wait for a rescue boat at Char Kazla in the Bogra district. Those who made it to higher ground shared the space with poisonous snakes, among other hazards.

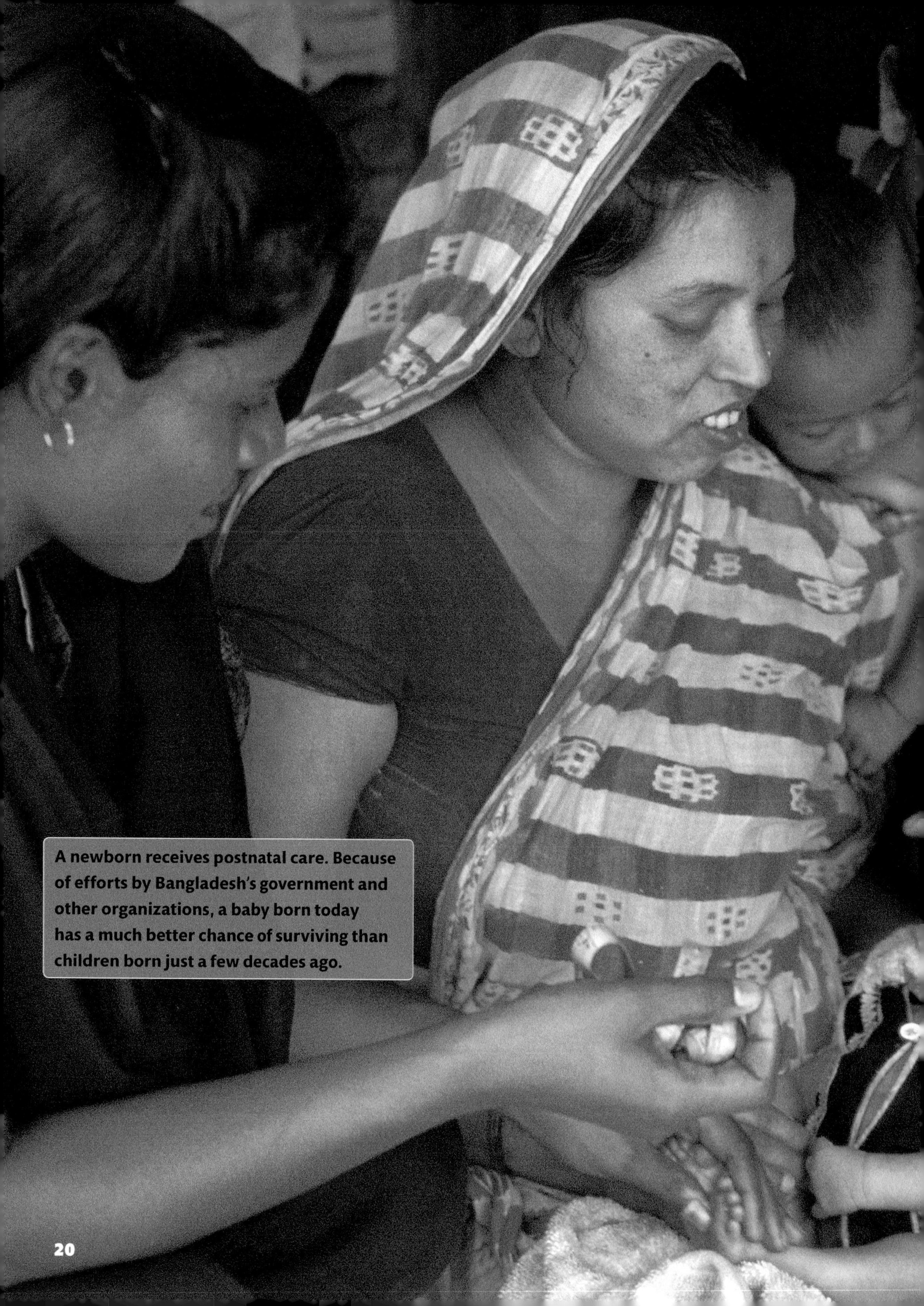

A newborn receives postnatal care. Because of efforts by Bangladesh's government and other organizations, a baby born today has a much better chance of surviving than children born just a few decades ago.

STRUGGLING IN THE SLUMS

Zaynab Begum and her family live in a slum in Dhaka, the most populated city in Bangladesh. There is no electricity, toilet, or running water. Zaynab and her family are among the millions of Bangladeshis who have moved from the countryside to the cities hoping for a better life. Some have come to find work. Others have migrated after floods or other natural disasters destroyed their farms.

Nearly 2,000 newcomers arrive in Dhaka each day. In 2010 the city's population reached more than 17 million, with nearly 60 percent of that number living in slums. By 2020 the population may top 20 million. Clearly something needs to be done.

WHAT TO DO

In the 1970s, the government created programs that helped lower the fertility rate from 6.6 children per woman in 1977 to about 2.4 today. Still, Bangladesh adds about three million people a year. Because 40 percent of the population is younger than 15, experts predict a new population boom when these youngsters begin having families.

One expert has suggested education as a possible solution. Bangladeshis who are trained in medicine or other professions can more easily **emigrate**, or move away, to other countries. Others propose relocating industries away from the cities to ease overcrowding.

While Bangladesh's government may be able to rein in population growth somewhat, one small country alone cannot reverse climate change. Rising waters may still force mass migrations. Still the Bangladeshis maintain a hopeful attitude.

"[Bangladeshis] may be poor . . . but we are not victims," says Zakir Kibria, a political scientist. "And when things get tough, people here do what they've always done—they find a way to adapt and survive."

Explore the Issue

1. **Compare and Contrast** How are Bangladesh's and South Korea's population issues similar and different?
2. **Draw Conclusions** How is climate change affecting the population of Bangladesh?

New Plants to feed the World

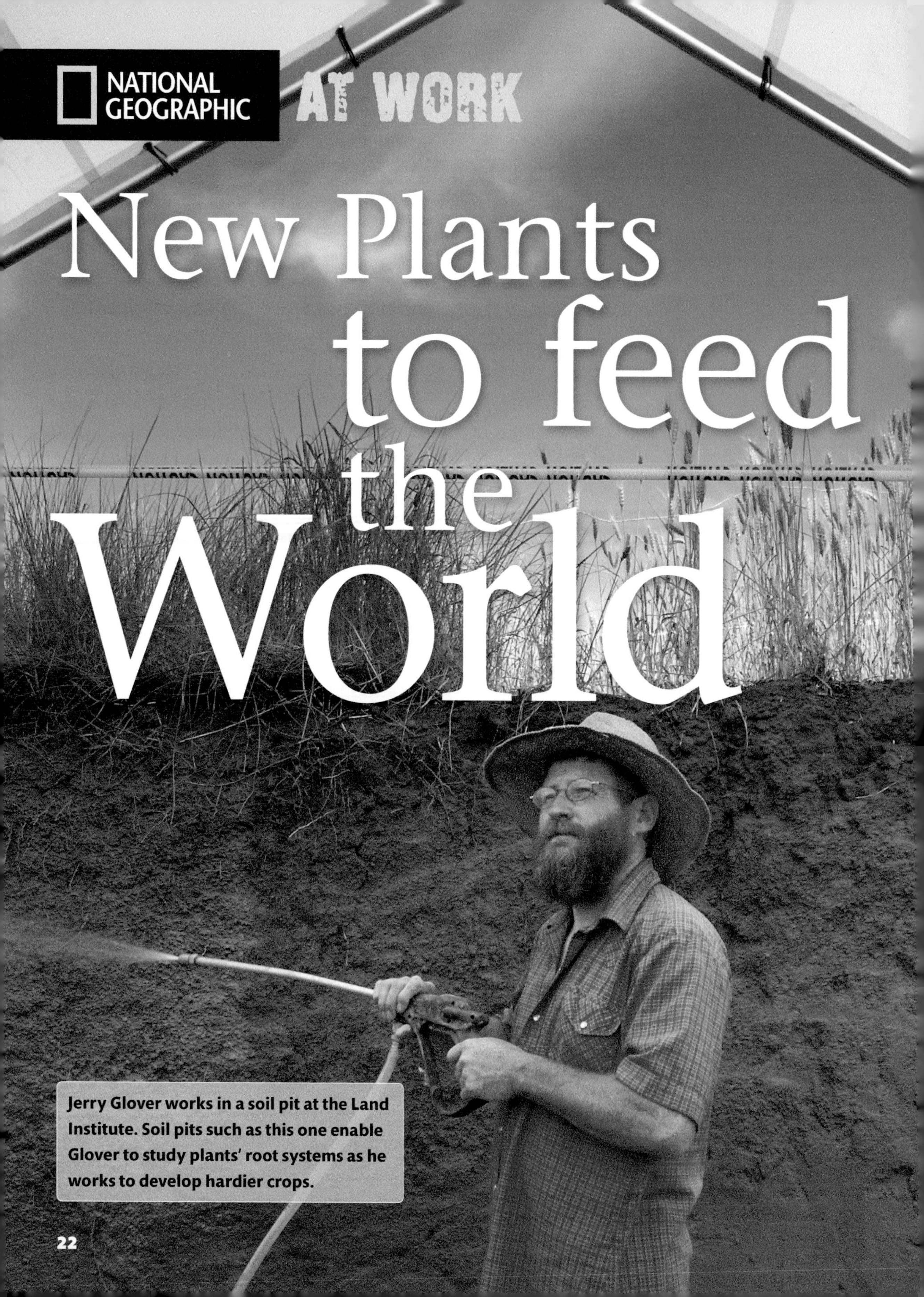

Jerry Glover works in a soil pit at the Land Institute. Soil pits such as this one enable Glover to study plants' root systems as he works to develop hardier crops.

FEEDING A HUNGRY WORLD

With the worldwide population at seven billion and growing, many experts are concerned about how the earth can provide enough food for so many people. Jerry Glover, a National Geographic Emerging Explorer, is among those working on the problem. Glover is an **agroecologist**, a scientist who studies farming's impact on the environment. Working with international agricultural organizations, Glover is looking for new ways to use perennial crops to feed people. He hopes to provide food for the one billion or so people who don't have enough to eat.

Glover's goal is to replace annual food crops, such as corn and wheat, with their perennial cousins. Annual plants grow, die, and then have to be planted again year after year. Perennial plants naturally resprout each year. Tulips and daffodils are common garden perennials. Some annual grains, such as wheat, have related perennial strains.

AN ANNUAL PROBLEM

Why does Glover want to replace annuals? While these crops can yield a bountiful harvest, they can also harm the planet. Annuals need large amounts of fertilizer and pesticides, which pollute the environment. In contrast, perennials use fewer chemicals and, with their deep root systems, hold onto the soil better than annuals. These roots protect against erosion, the gradual wearing away of the land.

Perennials such as these prairie plants have strong, deep roots that help preserve the land.

Planting perennials also means farmers will not have to gas up their tractors as often, thereby reducing the amount of **greenhouse gases** in the atmosphere. Greenhouse gases, such as carbon dioxide, contribute to climate change. Most importantly, because perennials have access to more water in the soil than annuals, they can grow in water-starved regions.

Overall, planting perennials promotes **sustainability**, which means carefully using resources in such a way that we do not deplete them. Sustainable farming practices allow people to grow crops without doing lasting damage to the land.

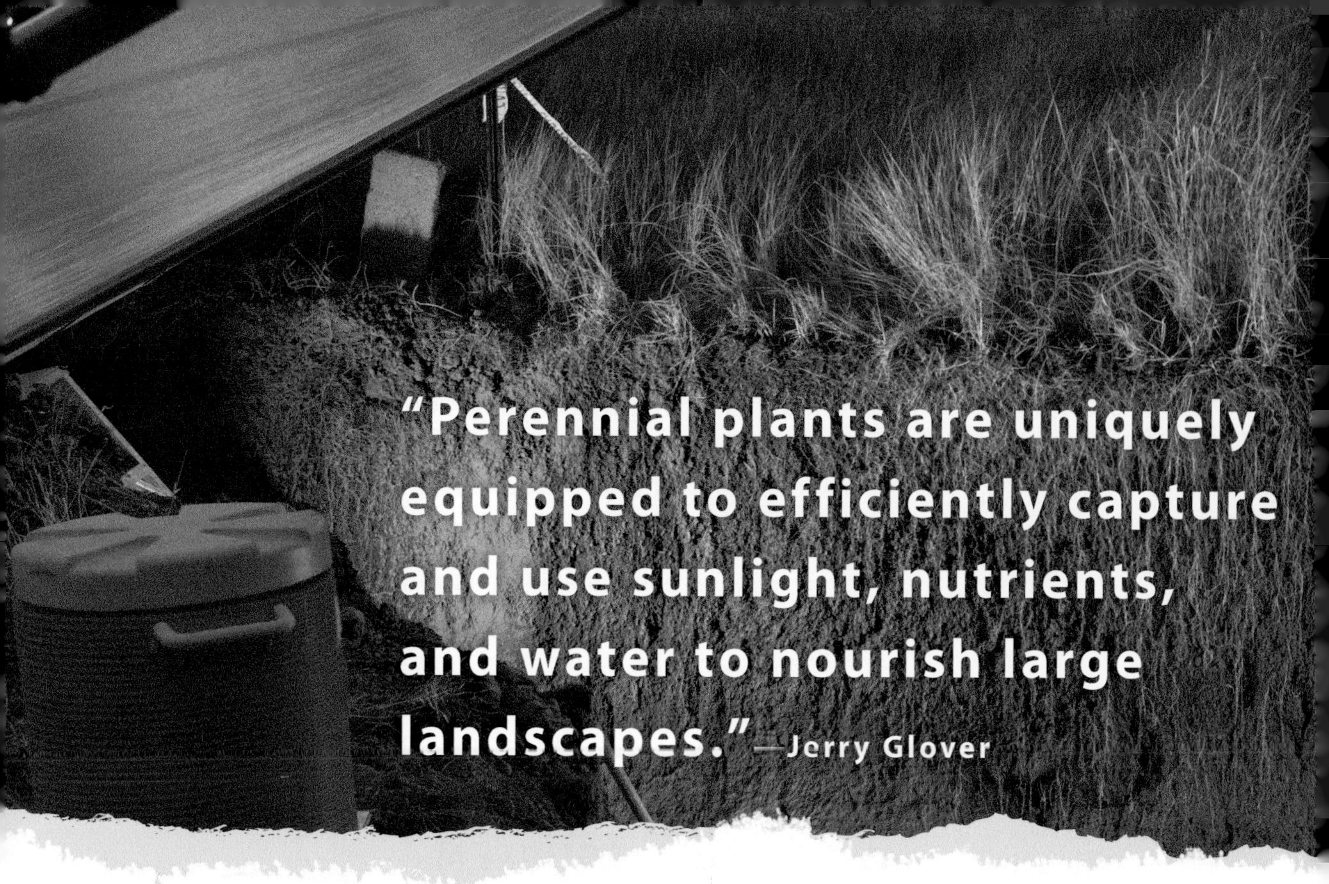

SEEKING A PERENNIAL SOLUTION

"Before agriculture, natural plant communities ruled the earth and kept ecosystems in balance," says Glover. "How? Those plants were perennials. Perennial plants are uniquely equipped to efficiently capture and use sunlight, nutrients, and water to nourish large landscapes." When humans started to settle down and begin farming, they replaced these plants with annuals that they grew for food. By choosing to replant only the seeds from the strongest plants, people could more easily modify annual crops to provide the best harvest.

Through the centuries, however, annual crops have continuously pulled water and nutrients from the soil, damaging the land. Glover and others are exploring ways to create perennial plants that allow farmers to create an abundant harvest while preserving the land.

The idea of replacing annual food crops with perennials is nothing new. It is, however, expensive and challenging work. For example, breeding a perennial corn crop that farmers can plant could cost more than $20 million.

This soil pit allows Jerry Glover to compare the root systems of two species side by side.

OVERCOMING THE OBSTACLES

As a scientist, Glover looks for ways to make perennials less expensive for farmers to plant, yet hardy enough to produce food at the same rate as annual crops. But perennials are stubborn. They use most of their energy to grow deep roots for a long life instead of producing seeds.

Despite these technical and financial drawbacks, Glover and other scientists are sure they can create perennial crops within 20 years that can help feed the world. "There is a growing international network of plant breeders working to solve this as the problems surrounding food production worsen," Glover says. If he is right, planting perennial crops could be the key to feeding the billions of people who will live on Earth in the future.

Explore the Issue

1. **Draw Conclusions** Why is it necessary to find alternative food sources to replace annual food crops?
2. **Identify Solutions** How can Glover's work help save the environment and solve the world's food crisis?

What Can I DO?

Take a Census

—and find out who lives in your community

To find out how many people live in an area, governments, including that of the United States, periodically take a census. A census records not only a country's population, but its diversity as well. A census is a good indicator of how a community changes over time. You can take a census too. You can then use that information to reach conclusions about a specific group.

IDENTIFY

- Decide whether to take a census of a school club, a community group, or any other group to which you belong.
- Choose a group that includes both males and females and people of different ages.
- Make sure the people in your group do not mind taking a few minutes to complete your census questionnaire.

ORGANIZE

- Prepare by explaining to the people in your group that you will be taking a census and by asking politely for their time.
- Focus on the ages and the genders of the population you are going to survey.
- Don't ask people their specific ages. Instead, give them a range to choose from, such as 10 to 15 years or 16 to 20 years.
- You should survey 15 to 20 people.

This teen is conducting a one-on-one interview to take her census.

DOCUMENT

- Create a questionnaire that you will copy and distribute.
- The questionnaire should ask people whether they are male or female.
- The questionnaire should also ask people to identify their age range.
- You may choose another question to ask, such as how often people use computers or other electronic devices.

SHARE

- Collect the questionnaires and tabulate, or organize, the results.
- Use pie charts or bar graphs to compare the age groups and numbers of males and females.
- Present your findings to your classmates. What conclusions can you draw from the data you collected?

Research & **WRITE**
Explanatory

Write an Explanatory Article

Changes in population can affect your neighborhood in ways you might not realize. Some communities grow so fast that they run short of water or land. In other areas, many people might move away, forcing schools and businesses to close. Write an article explaining how your community's growing or shrinking population has affected an aspect of life, such as energy use, water use, education, pollution, or housing.

RESEARCH

Use the library, the Internet, or newspapers to find out how changes in population have affected your community. You can also interview a knowledgeable person, such as a mayor or businessperson. Find out:

- if your community's population is increasing or declining;
- which aspect of life in your community has been most affected by population changes;
- what impact population changes have had on that aspect of your community's life.

Be careful to use only reliable sources.

DRAFT

Write a draft of the article. It should be at least three paragraphs long.

- The first paragraph should introduce your topic clearly. State how population change has affected an aspect of your community and preview what is to come in the article.
- The next paragraph or group of paragraphs should develop your topic with relevant facts, concrete details, examples, and definitions of population-related terms.
- Cite your sources accurately. Use direct quotes or paraphrase information.
- In the last paragraph, provide a concluding statement that supports your explanation of the impact of population change.

REVISE & EDIT

Exchange drafts with a partner. Consider the following questions and offer your comments to your partner.

- Does the introduction clearly state how one aspect of life in your community has been affected by population changes?
- Does the central section of the article support the topic with relevant, concrete details about your community?
- Does the concluding paragraph clearly support the explanation?

Revise the article to incorporate your partner's comments and your own ideas. The article should be clear, and its ideas should flow logically. Use appropriate transitions to show the relationships among ideas, and explain your topic with precise language. Check your paper for grammar, spelling, and punctuation.

PUBLISH & PRESENT

Break into groups of three or four. After reading each other's articles, discuss how population changes affect your community. Brainstorm some ideas to solve problems that may arise from these changes and present your findings to the class.

Visual GLOSSARY

agroecologist *n.*, a scientist who studies the impact of agriculture on the environment

climate change *n.*, the gradual increase in Earth's surface temperature

demographic change *n.*, change in the size and makeup of a country's population

emigrate *v.*, to leave one's country and move to another one

fertility rate *n.*, the average number of children born per woman in a population

greenhouse gas *n.*, gas, such as carbon dioxide, that is formed by burning fossil fuels such as oil and coal. Greenhouse gases contribute to climate change.

incentive *n.*, reward offered to influence people's behavior

migrate *v.*, to move from one region or country to another, often to seek work or other economic opportunities

pension plan *n.*, system in which people contribute money to a plan while they are working and receive payments from it when they retire

population *n.*, total number of people who occupy an area

sustainability *n.*, careful use of resources so that the resources are preserved and not depleted

agroecologist
migrate
population

INDEX

SKILLS